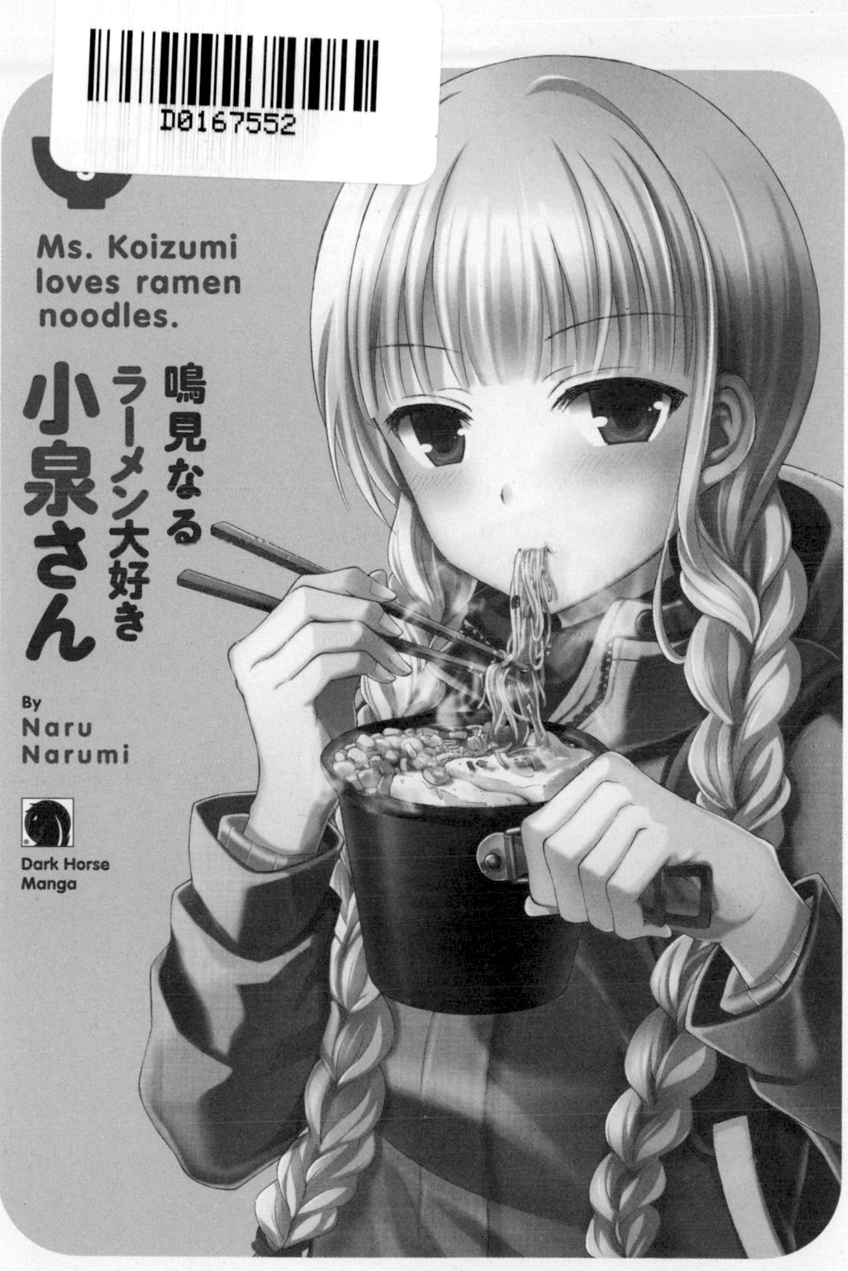

D0167552
Ms. Koizumi loves ramen noodles.
鳴見なる
ラーメン大好き
小泉さん
By
Naru Narumi
Dark Horse Manga

Ms. Koizumi loves ramen noodles.

# contents

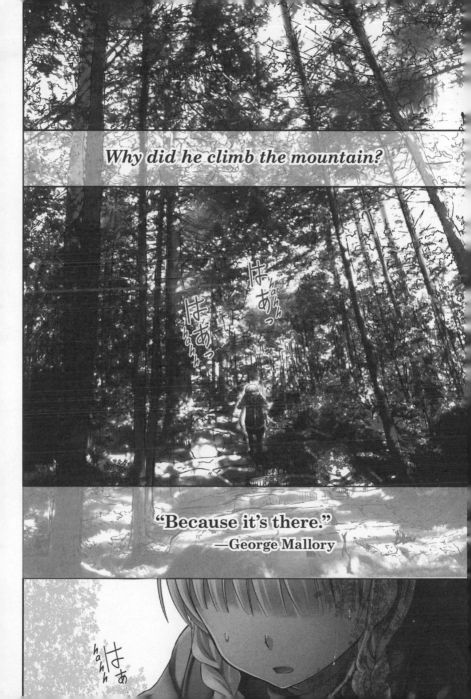

Why did he climb the mountain?
はあっ
はあっ
"Because it's there."
—George Mallory
はあ…

## 20th Bowl: Mountain

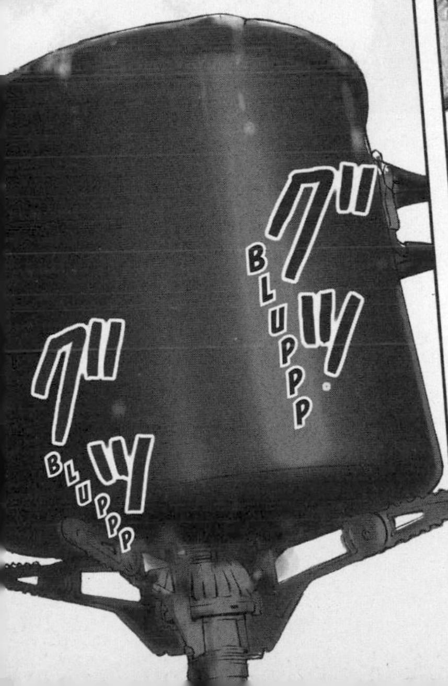
グツ
BLUPPP
グツ
BLUPPP

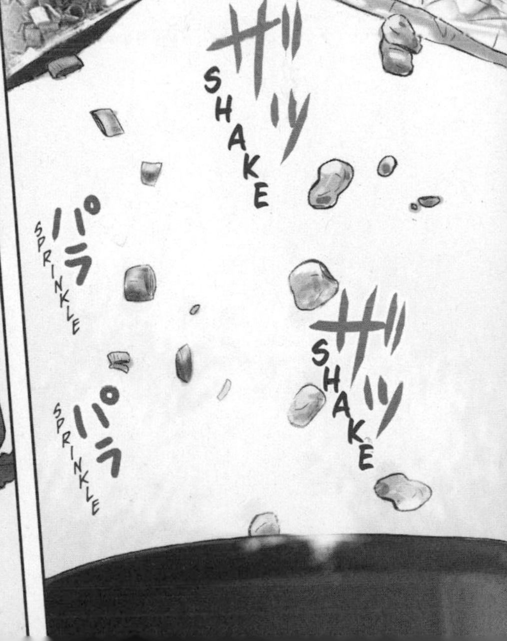
SHAKE
パラ
SPRINKLE
SHAKE
パラ
SPRINKLE

ふー
FWOOOOO
ふー
FWOOOOO

ずるっ
SLRRRPPP
ずずずっ
SLLRRPPPP
MUNCH
MUNCH
CHEW
ずるっ
SLLRRPP
ずずっ
SLLRRPPPP
ずずず。
SLLRRPPPPP
ずずっ
SLPP SLPP SLPP

ふはっ
SIGHHH...
ガラッ
RATTLE

はー
HAHHHHHHHH

ぎゅっ
TUG
Hello.
Hi.
はっ…
HAHH…
ごしっ
WIPE

HAHHHH
HAHHHH
...

The summit.

...EXCUSE ME, COULD YOU TAKE A PICTURE OF US?
DO YOU WANT ME TO TAKE A PICTURE OF YOU AT THE TOP OF MT. TSUKUBA, TOO?
I've got a Polaroid, too, if you'd prefer that.
NO, FOR YOU SEE...
KLICK
...
...MY GOAL LIES... FURTHER THAN THE SUMMIT.

*...what is further than the summit?*

ずずずっ
SLRPPPP
ずるっ
SLRPP
ずる
SLRPP

*Why did she climb the mountain?*

SIGH
"Because there's a ramen restaurant there."
—Ms. Koizumi

21st Bowl:
Back Fat
It is the guilty pleasures for which we most faithfully descend.
One will fall to them again—like the cherry blossoms, never learning to cling fast to the strong trunk of forbearance.

I WANT, I WANT...

...I WANT BACK FAT!
HAHH
TMP たっ
HAHH
TMP たっ

SPRING! FEWER LAYERS! LOSING WEIGHT!!
HUFF はっ
HUFF はっ
I, MISA NAKAMURA (16 YEARS OLD)...
...AM A BEAUTIFUL HIGH SCHOOL GIRL.
PANT! はっ
RECENTLY, I'VE BEEN DIETING WITHOUT TELLING ANYBODY.
はっ PANT!
たっ THMP
たーっ THMP
ドッ WHUDD
S...
...SORRY...
じっ STARE
OH, NO.

WRONG PERSON TO RUN INTO ...!
ZOOOOOM!
?
WHIRL!
JEEZ! I PICKED A FARAWAY NEIGHBOR-HOOD TO JOG...
...SHE'S THE LAST PERSON I EXPECTED TO SEE ME!

Eh ...?
...
WHO'S THAT MYSTERI-OUS GIRL...
Ah!
...WITH THE LOVELY COM-PLEXION ...?
SHINY!
SMOOTH!

DID SHE STAGE THIS JUST TO ANNOY ME ...?!
Don't get paranoid, Misa! She only outclasses you in ramen knowledge!!

STILL... MY SKIN'S GOTTEN BAD SINCE I STARTED THIS DIET...
...
GRIT!
GRIND!
I don't WANT to...
BUT I HAVE TO ASK HER...

IF YOU KNOW THE ENEMY AND KNOW YOURSELF, YOU NEED NOT FEAR THE RESULT OF A HUNDRED BATTLES!
—SUN TZU: ART OF WAR, CHAPTER 3, "ATTACK BY STRATAGEM"
HEY! KOIZUMI!
TELL ME...OF YOUR STRATAGEM!
GRAB
MY WHAT?
DON'T HOLD OUT ON ME! I KNOW!
YOU'RE DOING SOMETHING THESE DAYS! WHAT IS IT?!
ゆっさ SHAKE
ゆっさ SHAKE
?
A HINT IS FINE! JUST TELL ME!!
I WON'T SETTLE FOR A HINT!
...
UM...

Doing something? These days?

...

WELL, I'VE BEEN...

EATING RAMEN.

Why did I even ask?

THANK YOU FOR WAITING!

Here's your usual, miss.

sigh

WELL, JUST A BOWL SHOULD BE FINE. I'LL CALL THIS A CHEAT DAY.

I've had nothing but salad this week.

Well, these scallions are vegeta-bles...

...?

ALL OVER THIS SOUP... THERE'S SOMETHING THAT LOOKS LIKE FLOATING PETALS.
OH, THAT'S JUST THE BACK FAT.
THE BACK...
...FAT ?!

Um...

FAT. YOU DID SAY *"FAT,"* RIGHT?

NOT, "YO, THIS IS PHAT?" THEY'RE PRO-NOUNCED THE SAME.

*Oh.*

MAYBE YOU SHOULDN'T TOUCH THE OUTSIDE OF THE BOWL.

*It's oily.*

EVEN THE *BOWL* IS FAT?!

CHA チャッ CHA チャッ

THE LARD IS HEATED UNTIL SOFT, AND THEN SPRINKLED ONTO THE SOUP THROUGH A STRAINER.

IT'S CALLED *SEABURA CHA CHA*—BACK FAT CHA-CHA STYLE.

*Thank you for the meal.*

*This process makes the soup richer and milder.*

IT'S BECOME AN ADDICTION OF MINE RECENTLY.

IT'S LIKE A SLICK, SLIPPERY DOWNWARD SPIRAL FOR ME-- A SPIRAL... GREASED WITH BACK FAT.

ギトー GOOOOOOOEY

WHAT WILL IT *DO* TO ME?

*It certainly sounds scary.*

SIGHHH

つやぁぁぁぁ

SHI-I-I-INNNE

うぐ...

GULP...

WHAT IS THIS ....?
I'VE NEVER HAD SUCH RAMEN !!!
IT'S RICH... BUT IT'S NOT AS HEAVY AS IT LOOKS!
How is this pos-sible ?!
ONE...
...ONE MORE BITE.
SLRRRPPP
Oh, no.
I CAN'T STOP ....!
I SHOULD STOP...
GRAB

BUT...
I...
...CAN'T STOP !!!

I ATE IT ALL...
AND...
...I GIVE UP.
KOI-ZUMI...
...GUIDE ME FURTHER DOWN THE SPIRAL.

*Next day*

*Three days later*

*Five days later*

HERE'S YOUR BOWL-- SUPER GOOEY!

こってりらーめん

ずるっ SLRPPP

ずるっ SLRRPP

ずるっ SLRRPP

SLRPPPP
ずずず...
☒ Hirataishu Asian (Os
☒ Gottsu (Akihabara)
☒ Yamate Ramen (Komab
☒ Konjiki Hototogisu (Shin
☒ Gedobashi Ramen (Tokiw
☒ Ramen Kazuki (Roppon


*One week later*

ARE THERE MORE PLACES TO VISIT, KOIZUMI...?
OH, YES.
営業中


HERE'S YOUR BOWL-- ULTRA GOO... FOR TWO!

Let me know if you need more fat!

CRYSTAL BITS OF LARD FALL...

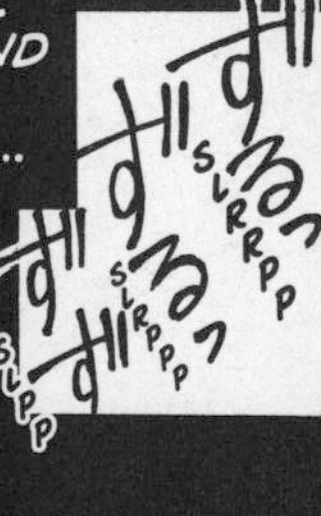

...ALL AROUND MY HEAD...

...AND IN THE WIND.


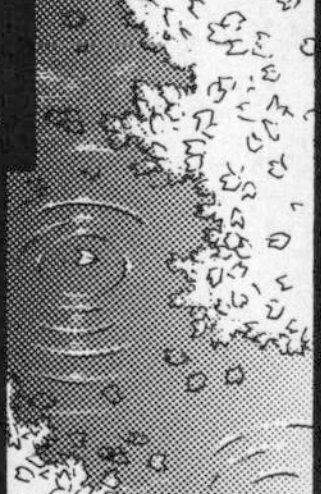

HEY, COULD I HAVE EXTRA FAT?

Do you know the warning signs of back fat addiction?
But it's perfectly legal, you know.
Yes. Super. Ultra.
Koizumi, are you gonna get super fat again today?
dazed

**Ms. Koizumi loves ramen noodles**

MMM...
IT'S THE TASTE...
...JUST NOW...

22nd Bowl:
Euglena

...OF
MILLIONS
OF
EUGLENA
IN MY
BODY!

EUGLENA!

I LOOKED THEM UP.

THEY'RE A GENUS OF MICROSCOPIC CREATURES WHICH ARE ABOUT 0.05MM IN SIZE!

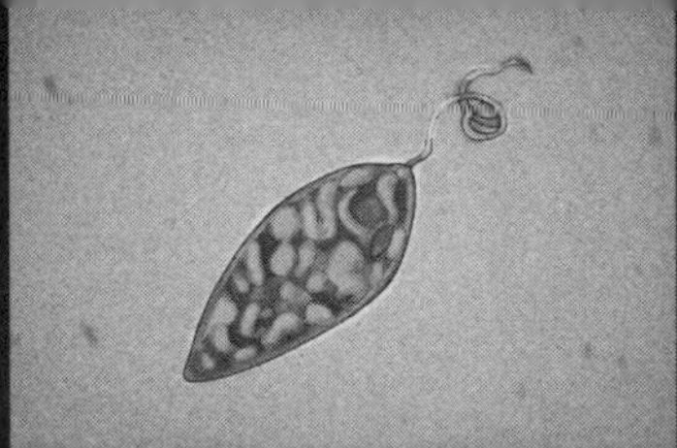

THEY CONTAIN DOZENS OF NUTRIENTS...

...AND THESE DAYS THEY'RE A POPULAR HEALTHY "SUPERFOOD"!

CHECK *THIS* OUT!

EUGLENA SWEETS!

I HEAR THEY'RE GOOD FOR YOUR *BEAUTY!*

BUT THEY'RE *BUGS!*
MISA, YOU DON'T LIKE BUGS.
*I don't think you can eat them.*
DON'T YOU KNOW EUGLENA *MEANS* "BEAUTY"? FOR BEAUTY, I'D EAT A MILLION BUGS!
SWEEP
SWEEP
...
*HA! THEY'RE NOT BUGS, THEY'RE A UNICELLULAR ORGANISM! WE LEARNED THAT IN CLASS.*
*Although you probably forgot it, Yu.*
*mutter*
AND YET, I'M CURIOUS HOW THEY TASTE...
*hmm hmm*
SWEEP
SWEEP

...IT ALSO DOESN'T MEAN "BEAUTY." IT MEANS "GOOD EYEBALL."
MUMBLE
MUMBLE
MUTTER
BUT IT'S NOT A GOOD EYEBALL, THOUGH. IT'S MORE OF A PHOTO-RECEPTIVE ORGAN-ELLE.
...OH.
AND... HERE WE ARE.
UM...
...I'M NOT EVEN SURE IF I TASTED THE EUGLENA.
It was just like pesto flavored ramen.
Today I spoiled myself. Extra euglena.
SLRPP
SLRPP
YEAH. THAT'S WHAT EUGLENA TASTE LIKE.
BUT IF YOU FEEL YOU'RE NOT TASTING THEM, I KNOW A PLACE WHERE THEY MAKE THE NOODLES OUT OF EUGLENA, NOT JUST THE SOUP.
We need only hop on the subway.
Eh?
UM, I DON'T KNOW...
I mean...
...I'VE ALREADY HAD 600 MILLION TODAY.

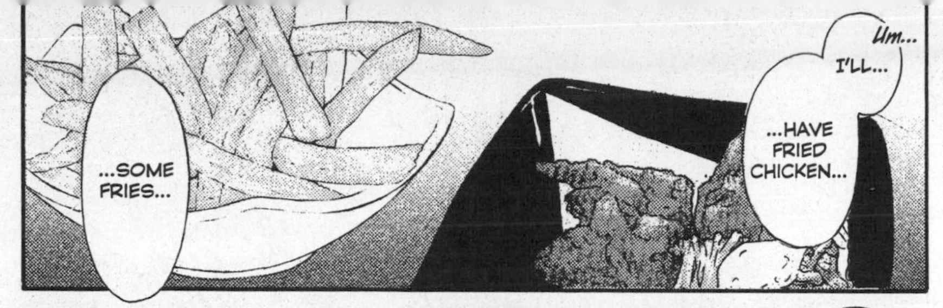


...A BIT OF COD ROE SALAD...

...A MILLE CREPE...

...OH! AND WATER-MELON ...!

...

REALLY, YU...?

ザワ YAMMER!

THIS IS A SUSHI RESTAURANT, YOU KNOW...!

So maybe you should order some sushi...?

ザワ YAMMER!

TODAY MY BROTHER WILL TREAT ME TO DINNER (WHICH DOESN'T HAPPEN OFTEN)!

He just got paid from his part-time job.

ガヤ CHAT!

ガヤ CHAT!

23rd Bowl: Rolling Ramen

Yay!

EGG SUSHI!

It's my favor-ite!

YOU'RE SUCH A *CHILD!*

Eat fish!

EH? BUT *YOU* GOT TUNA MAYO SUSHI! THAT'S FOR KIDS TOO!

AT LEAST IT'S FISH.

And it's MY favorite.

By the way...
...IT'S VERY SWEET OF YOU TO BUY SIS DINNER, BUT WHY ME AND NOT YOUR GIRLFRIEND?
SMIRK
SMIRK
OH, RIGHT... YOU DON'T *HAVE* A GIRLFRIEND... AND NEVER *HAVE* HAD A GIRL-FRIEND!
Hey...
...I JUST HAD A THOUGHT. WHY DON'T WE GO DUTCH?
SORRY, BROTHER, I WAS JUST KIDDING! ♡

Well, then, I should get salmon next... since we are in a sushi restaurant.
...
...?!

...MS. KOIZUMI?!

WHAT'S MS. KOIZUMI DOING IN A SUSHI TRAIN RESTAURANT...?
They don't specialize in ramen!
DO YOU KNOW HER?
Y-Y-Y-YES!
We're rather close, actually!


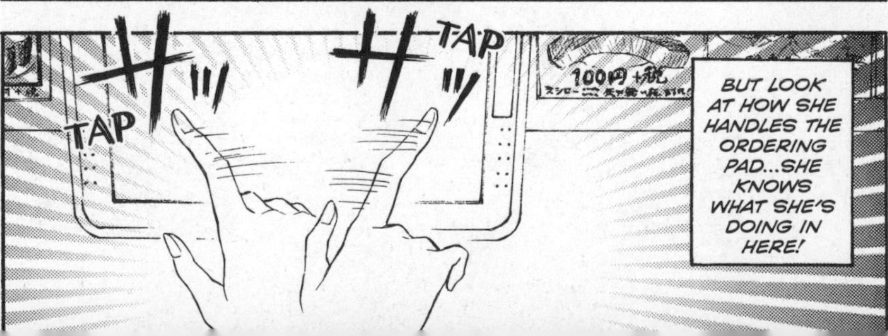

BUT LOOK AT HOW SHE HANDLES THE ORDERING PAD...SHE KNOWS WHAT SHE'S DOING IN HERE!
100円+税
TAP
TAP

TUNK
FULL COURSE
ROAST PORK WITH TONS OF SCALLION
MEDIUM FATTY TUNA
SALMON ROE
?
B-but what's in the bowl...?
STEAM
GRIP

YES! IT'S RAMEN!

I had my suspicions...

RAMEN

ちゅるるっ

SLRRRPP

SUSHI

はふっ

CHOMP

RAMEN

ずるるる

SLRRPP

SUSHI

RAMEN

I...I UNDER-STAND NOW...!
IT'S NOT ABOUT WHETHER THE RESTAURANT SPECIALIZES IN RAMEN OR NOT... IT'S ABOUT ENJOYING RAMEN AT ANY KIND OF RESTAURANT THAT SERVES IT! YES! THE RAMEN, OF COURSE...BUT ALSO THE PAIRING OF THE RAMEN! SHE'S EXPERIENCING A UNIQUE RAMEN/SUSHI SYNERGY AT THIS VERY MOMENT...!
SEE, BY NOW I CAN TELL ALL THAT JUST BY WATCHING THE BACK OF HER HEAD.
I WANT TO TALK TO HER... BUT I'LL JUST WATCH FOR NOW....
NOD
NOD
STARE...

じ
STARE
!!
MY BRO!

STARE
Don't...
...DON'T TELL ME HE'S INTO HER, TOO ...?

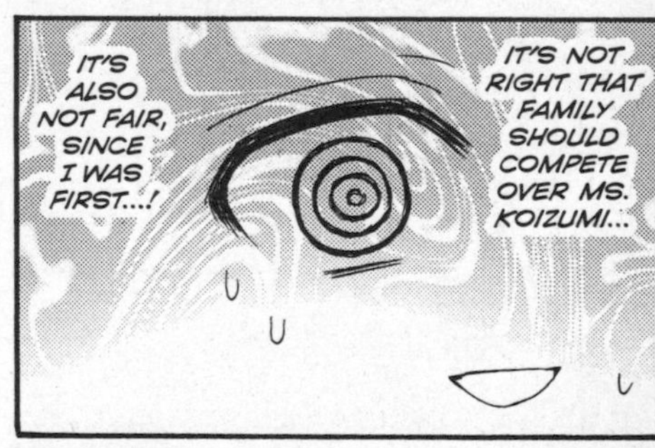
IT'S NOT RIGHT THAT FAMILY SHOULD COMPETE OVER MS. KOIZUMI...
IT'S ALSO NOT FAIR, SINCE I WAS FIRST...!

Y-YOU'RE STARING AT HER...
...S-SO HUNGRILY...
HEY!

LET'S HAVE SOME... *RAMEN!*
It looks good.
WHADDYA THINK?
*EHH ...?*

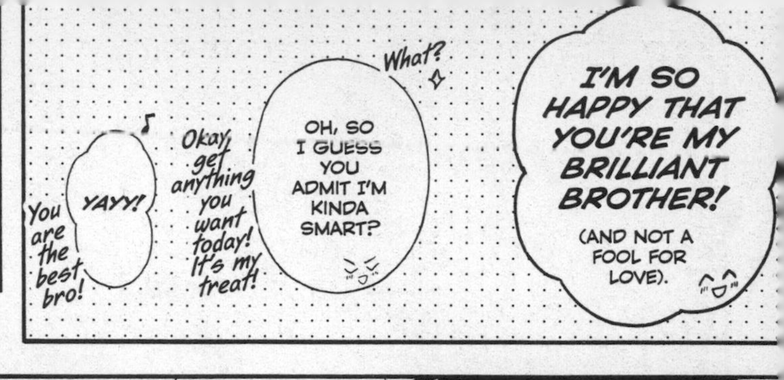


Thanks for the meal...!

It's the Sweets of the Week!
LIVE
24th Bowl: Long Line
JUST LOOK AT THIS LINE...!
THESE SWEETS ARE THE HOTTEST TREAT IN TOKYO THIS WEEK...
TV

SO, YEAH, WE HAD TO WAIT IN LINE FOR THREE HOURS, BUT...
Ehh ...?
WOW, UNBELIEVABLE...
990

...WE'RE GONNA SHOW OFF AT SCHOOL TOMORROW! ♪
It's the Sweets of the Week!
...I DON'T GET HOW PEOPLE DO THAT.
Say...
...MS. KOIZUMI, DO YOU WAIT IN LINES THAT LONG SOMETIMES FOR RAMEN ...?

I DON'T LIKE BEING IN LONG LINES.
I avoid it whenever I can.
Ehhhh?
REALLY?
I didn't expect that!
I FIGURED BY NOW THAT SHE'D ENDURE ANY WAIT FOR RAMEN...
...Wait!
ON THE OTHER HAND, SHE'D KNOW ALL THE OBSCURE PLACES THAT ARE GOOD.
She doesn't need to wait in line at those trendy places...

It's got to move soon!

It's crazy!

Yeah...

I'm in line...

SO HOT...

Whew...

♪

Sighhh...

About one more hour...

Don't you think?

IT'S VITAL RE-SEARCH...

MS. KOIZUMI IS PLANNING TO COME TO THIS SHOP WHICH ALWAYS HAS A LONG LINE.

BUT TODAY SHE HAS SOME AFTER SCHOOL CLASS-WORK...

OH, THE WAY SHE SAID, "I DON'T LIKE BEING IN LONG LINES"...

...BUT IT SEEMS SHE GOES FOR FADS AFTER ALL.

NEXT IN LINE!

That's cute, though.

Okay!

ふふふ CHUCKLE

HEAT WAVE

Ah!

FINALLY I'VE GOT TO HALFWAY!

ゾロ INCH

Hur-ry!

ゾロ INCH

ウロ FIDGET

ウロ FIDGET

Are you close?

スッ SLIP

While you're wait-ing, here's a menu.

Ah, thanks.

WOWWWWW!

THIS SHOP HAS MY FAVORITE TONKOTSU RAMEN!

It looks so good!

...

1130円

80

I SHOULD COME BACK HERE FOR REAL NEXT TIME...!
I wanna try it!
HEY-YYY!
ABOUT TIME! OVER HERE!

HOW LONG DID IT TAKE YOU TO SHOW UP, ANYWAY ...?
Come on, dudes.
SORRY, SORRY!
Sorry.
You got us a good spot in line!
IT WAS SO HOT...
...SO WE WERE IN STAR-BUCKS! ♪
!

SQUEEZE
UH, HEY, HIGH SCHOOL GIRL.
Could you please move back a bit, so...?
EH? Uh...
...WAIT, WHAT?
?!

ISN'T THAT... CHEAT-ING?
EHHHHHH?!
Um...
EXCUSE ME...
...BUT I DON'T THINK IT'S FAIR THAT YOU GUYS CUT IN LINE.
NOD うんうん NOD
WHAT? BUT I WAS IN LINE THE WHOLE TIME!
I HAD TO HOLD THIS PLACE FOR ALMOST AN HOUR IN THIS HEAT!
It's not an easy job, girl.
But...
...WE'VE ALL BEEN WAITING IN THE SAME HEAT...!
This isn't just about me!
Yep. yep.
SO EVERYONE CAN SEE THEY'RE GUILTY, BUT THEY'RE JUST GOING TO GET AWAY WITH IT...?
Oh...
...WELL, COULD YOU JUST LET IT SLIDE FOR TODAY, THOUGH ...?
JUST TODAY, I WON'T DO IT AGAIN, YOU KNOW!
I won't do it again.

YES, WHAT *ARE* YOU DOING ...?

...MS. KOI-ZUMI!

IT'S UNSEEMLY TO MAKE A SCENE OUTSIDE A SHOP OR RESTAU-RANT.

And I'm not sure why you're here in the first place.

Please!
LISTEN TO ME, MS. KOI-ZUMI!
たたたっ
SCAMPER
I...
...I WAS HOLDING YOUR SPOT! THAT'S WHY I'M HERE.

IT'S ALSO RUDE TO CUT IN LINE.
ギロッ
GLARE
I-I KNOW, BUT...

...It's not like that!
YOU WOULDN'T HAVE BEEN CUTTING IN...
...I was going to leave and let you have my place!
Is she a gofer?
What?
Huh...
I SEE.
BUT SOME PEOPLE WOULD CUT IN LINE INADVERTENTLY, WITHOUT THINKING ABOUT IT, IF THEY WERE JUST IN A SMALL GROUP.
This problem happens often for the popular places!

*Right...*

AND THEN THERE ARE A FEW PEOPLE WHO'D DO IT EVEN *IF* THEY THOUGHT ABOUT IT...

チラッ GLANCE

チラッ GLANCE

?

I DON'T THINK SO.

NO TRUE RAMEN LOVER COULD ACT LIKE SUCH TRASH.

ACTUALLY, THEY COULD...

*...they love this ramen...*

THEY *DON'T* LOVE RAMEN. SUCH PEOPLE DON'T *EXIST*.

BECAUSE I WAS DRIVEN BY MY IMPULSE.

I JUST HAD TO EAT THIS RA-MEN...
...NOW...
...AT ANY COST.

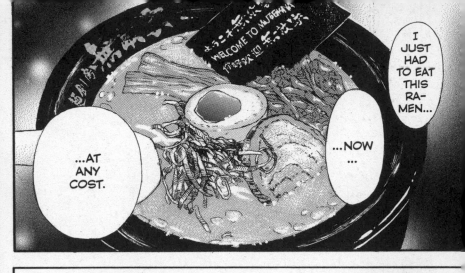

ONCE YOU FEEL THAT WAY...
...THERE IS NO CHOICE BUT TO PERSEVERE, NO MATTER HOW LONG THE RAMEN MAY TARRY.

...
Um...
IS IT THAT GOOD?
This ramen?
YEAH, I LIKE IT A LOT.
I see, I get it.

Before we get in line, let's take a picture of the line at our back!
Memory of our trip!
I started a new blog about popular food...
...so I want to take a picture of this line.
Yeah, it's been already two hours...
No, it's nothing. During the holiday last week...
...I waited for four hours...

...
I GUESS THERE ARE SOME PEOPLE WHO JUST REALLY WANT TO WAIT IN A LINE.
...

THAT'S ONE WAY OF ENJOYING RAMEN.

IN THE END, IT DOESN'T REALLY MATTER...
...WHY OR HOW YOU GET TO A GOOD RAMEN PLACE.
JUST ENJOYING GOOD RAMEN IS WHAT MATTERS MOST.
Mmm!
YEAH, THAT MAKES SENSE!
2 hours later
Ah, so good...!
ふは
WHEWWWW...
So happy.
Yu's now not only into ramen, but also waiting in ramen lines.
LET'S WAIT IN LINE AND GET THAT RAMEN AGAIN!
Tonkotsu, garlic, pickled mustard leaves!
WHY NOT GO BY YOURSELF?
WAITING TWO HOURS BY MYSELF AND WAITING TWO HOURS WITH *YOU* ARE VERY DIFFERENT EXPERIENCES!

HOME EC
BLUPP
BLUPP
25th Bowl:
Delicious Ramen
UMM...
...I THOUGHT IT WAS A BIT SWEETER.
Should I add more sugar?
YU! ENOUGH! STOP USING US AS YOUR TASTE-TESTERS!
Ehhhh?
HOW ABOUT JUST ONE MORE BOWL?
NO.
Thanks any-way.
I THINK IT TASTES FINE AS IT IS.
What are you trying to accom-plish?
NO! IT'S STILL NOT QUITE RIGHT!

WHEN I WAS LITTLE, I HAD A REALLY DELICIOUS BOWL OF RAMEN IN OSAKA.

I think it was close to my grand-ma's house.

LAST NIGHT, SUDDENLY, I REMEMBERED ABOUT IT...

It's so good...

...Yum-my!

I WANTED TO RECREATE THAT RAMEN AND USE IT TO WIN OVER MS. KOIZUMI.

Yes, what an amazing person you are, making this ramen! Let's be friends!

I would LOVE to!

I don't think...

...It would be that easy...

But...

...IT'S HARD TO MAKE THE EXACT SAME BOWL, THOUGH. MY MEMORY FROM BACK THEN IS PRETTY VAGUE.

Well...

...DO YOU REMEMBER THE SHOP? WHERE IT WAS?

NOTHING.

I was too young.

And it's not like I can take her to Osaka to hunt around for it...

HMMM...

WELL, THEN...

...WHY DON'T YOU ASK YOUR BROTHER? HE MIGHT KNOW.

No wonder you're class rep!

GOOD IDEA, JUN!

ピロン
BEEP
Your sister?
AH?
IT'S FROM YU.

YU
Bro, I need your help ASAP. Do you remember the ramen we had in Osaka a long time ago? The ramen shop we went to with the family around the time I was in kinder-garten?
YU
What was that ramen?
LET ME KNOW!
...
YEAH.

YU
I'm not asking what you thought about it. (˙_˙)

HUH!
WHAT A JERK, YU!
I just TOLD you...!
Why so upset, Osawa?
Sib-lings.

I can't ask him...
...I NEED TO FIGURE IT OUT BY MY-SELF!

I THINK THERE WERE SOME LEAFY GREENS AND GROUND MEAT....
It was kind of like a hot pot.
And...
...THE SOUP HAD A BIT OF SWEET MILD FLAVOR LIKE SUKIYAKI...
But...
...THE FLAVOR WASN'T AS LIGHT.
うーーん
UMMMMMMMMOOO
It was just...
...SUCH A DELI-CIOUS RAMEN.
I THINK YOU'LL NEED MORE TO GO ON THAN THAT.
mutter
DELI-CIOUS RAMEN...
GASP!
びくっ
STARE
MS. KOIZUMI ...?!

Excuse me...

...I DON'T MEAN TO INTRUDE...

MUMBLE

...BUT I SMELLED RAMEN, SO I HAD TO CHECK.

MUMBLE

Um...

...THAT'S ALL RIGHT, COME ON IN!

THE RAMEN YOU WERE DESCRIBING...

...I THINK IT'S *DELICIOUS* RAMEN.

Wow.

She was lured in.

Maybe Yu's plan will work.

?

YES, IT WAS DELICIOUS...

BUT YOU CAN GET IT IN TOKYO, YOU KNOW...

!

You can?!

Have a good time, you two.

Yeah. We've had enough ramen today.

ラーメン
おいしい ラーメン
入口

4 煮玉子ねぎ
A soft-boiled egg, green onions noodle
¥930
OISHII ...?
"DELICIOUS" ...?!
10
Bean Ve
oodles
730
9 おいしいラーメン
Oishii noodle
¥730
ラーメン
e) noodle
030
330
24
25
26
27
入口
ENTRANCE
THANK YOU FOR WAITING ...!
SO HE WAS TRYING TO TELL ME IT WAS CALLED "DELICIOUS"...
I gotta apologize to my bro...

HERE'S YOUR "DELICIOUS RAMEN"!

ふぁ～
AAAAHH
Just as I remem-bered!
あああ
HHHHHHHH!

THIS IS IT! THIS MILD SWEETNESS FROM NAPA CABBAGE...
But it's not too bland. Maybe it's because there's some extra flavored oil...
They always serve it very hot.
ふー
FOOOO
ふー
FOOOO
ふー
FOOOO

ずるっ
SLRRPPP
ずずずっ
SLRRRPPPPP

ごくっ
GULP
ぐいぐい
GULLPP
GULLPP

IT REALLY WAS...

...SO DELICIOUS!!!

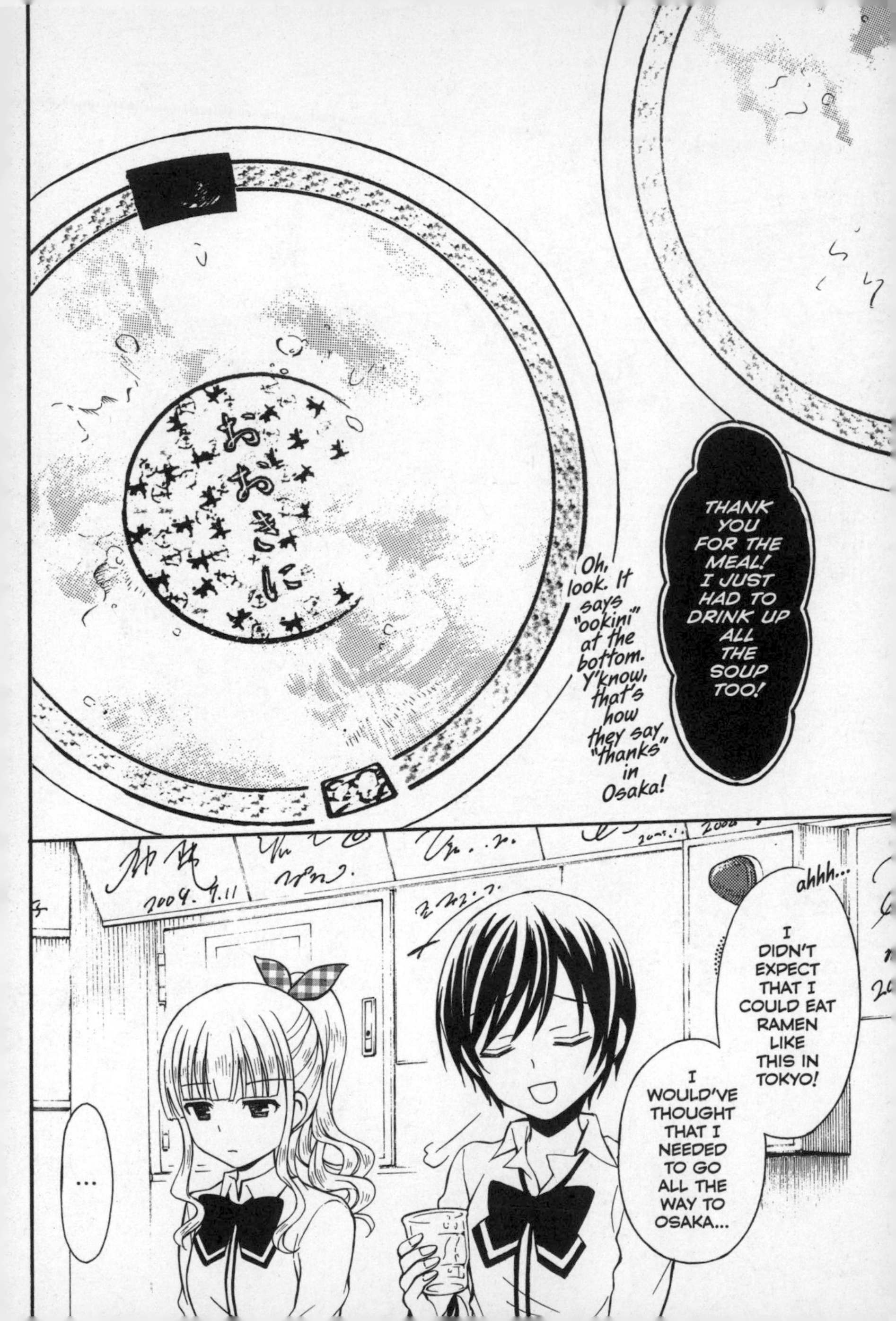
THANK YOU FOR THE MEAL! I JUST HAD TO DRINK UP ALL THE SOUP TOO!
Oh, look. It says "ookini" at the bottom. Y'know, that's how they say "thanks" in Osaka!
おおきに
ahhh...
I DIDN'T EXPECT THAT I COULD EAT RAMEN LIKE THIS IN TOKYO!
I WOULD'VE THOUGHT THAT I NEEDED TO GO ALL THE WAY TO OSAKA...
...

?

MS. KOIZUMI ...?

— Next day —

ONE TICKET TO OSAKA, PLEASE. ON THE BULLET TRAIN.

乗車券・新幹線自由席特急券 ****

東 京（都区内）→新大阪（市内）

5月　日から　乗車券4日間・自由席券2日間有効

¥13.240 内訳：乗8.510・特4.730

TAITO STATION
precia
docomo
26th Bowl:
Osaka
HIC

...
ちゅるっ
SLRPP
は
HAHHHHHHHH...
ザ
SSSHHHHH...
...

CLINCH!

SORRY I WAS LATE, CHARLOTTE!

THANK YOU FOR WAITING!

!

LET'S GO, OKAY?
TUG
TUG
?
?
Wait for me!

UM... WHO'S "CHAR-LOTTE"?
AND WHO ARE YOU?
I MADE IT UP.
YOU KIND OF LOOK LIKE A "CHAR-LOTTE," THOUGH.
SLIP

...

...THANK YOU FOR YOUR HELP.
Hold on a sec!
DIDN'T I SEE YOU HAVING RAMEN IN NAMBA LAST NIGHT...?

JUDGING BY YOUR ACCENT, I GUESSED YOU WERE FROM TOKYO...

Plus...
...AFTER YOU ATE, YOU PUT YOUR BOWL BACK ON THE COUNTER.
You don't see that much around here.
It's OK, leave it there.
Sorry, it's my habit.

ARE YOU IN HIGH SCHOOL?
IS THIS A TRIP BY YOURSELF ...?

...
I CAME HERE TO EAT RAMEN.

Um...
...SPEAKING AS A LOCAL MYSELF...
...OSAKA ISN'T A BIG PLACE FOR RAMEN, YA KNOW?
WE DON'T HAVE ANY LOCAL STYLES.
Is it really worth coming all the way from Tokyo?
YOU ARE MISINFORMED.

OSAKA IS...
...A HOT TOWN FOR RAMEN!!

YOUR OLD SHOPS ARE STILL GOOD...
...BUT ALSO THERE ARE ALSO SO MANY UP-AND COMING RAMEN PLACES IN OSAKA THESE DAYS.
YOU JUST SAID THAT OSAKA HAS NO LOCAL RAMEN, BUT...
...WERE YOU NOT AWARE OF THE "TAKAIDA STYLE" ...?
Those Chinese noodles (chuka soba) you watched me eat last night were in the Takaida style.
HIGH WATER RATIO, THICK NOODLES
+
A THICK SOY SAUCE BASE
And...
...MY FAVORITE IS THE RAMEN DERIVED FROM TAKAIDA STYLE SOY SAUCE (SHOYU RAMEN)... "OSAKA BLACK."
SILENCE
ポカン…
GASP
はっ

THIS IS MY LAST DAY IN OSAKA.
...BUT!
OFF I GO, THEN.
I want to get in at least 4 more bowls.
Um...
HeYYY! HeYYY!
Hey, where you going?
WHOOSH
...
Blocked.
I knew it.
OH, WELL...
sad
Say...
...HOW'S ABOUT THIS?
...LET BIG SIS HERE BE YOUR BODYGUARD...
...AND ESCORT YOU ON THE LAST DAY OF YOUR RAMEN TOUR IN OSAKA ...!
HeYYY!
HeYYY!
HeYYY!
...

...
Nice!
MY NAME IS AYANE!
HOW 'BOUT YOU?
25 Years old.
IT'S A DEAL.
I'M KOI-ZUMI.
KOI-ZUMI-CHAN!
Nice to meet you!
GRAB
...
WHO DOES SHE REMIND ME OF ...?
Nice to meet you!
はっ hahh
はっ hahh
WELL, I'M GLAD WE MET...
...BECAUSE I WANTED A FINAL FEAST IN OSAKA BEFORE I LEFT.
THIS IS MY LAST DAY HERE AS WELL.
?

ONE *TORIPAITAN*—CHICKEN WHITE SOUP...
...AND ONE *GOKUNOU TORIPAITAN*—SUPER RICH CHICKEN WHITE SOUP. THANK YOU FOR WAITING!
IT'S LIKE IT'S BURIED IN *HOT SNOW*!!!
It's so white there's a glare...
WAIT, WEREN'T YOU TALKING ABOUT WANTING THE OSAKA BLACK STYLE JUST A LITTLE WHILE AGO...?
I ALREADY HIT MOST OF THE TRADITIONAL PLACES FOR BLACK RAMEN YESTERDAY.
SO I'M MAINLY TRYING NEWER SHOPS TODAY.
PLUS...

...IN OSAKA, THE HOT STYLES THESE DAYS ARE WHITE RAMEN LIKE *TORIPAITAN*... (CHICKEN WHITE SOUP)

...AND ALL THE KINDS OF SALT RAMEN VARIETIES.

塩
専門
NAMBA
THAT *TORIPAITAN* WAS SO MILKY...!
Actually...
...IT'S NOT WHITE FROM MILK.
In general.
EH ?!
Really?!
YOU GET THE *PAITAN* WHITE SOUP FROM COOKING IT AT HIGH HEAT FOR A LONG TIME...
...BUT IF YOU SIMMER IT AT LOW HEAT FOR A LONG TIME, THEN YOU GET A CLEAR SOUP... *CHINTAN*.
I see. I didn't know that high school in Tokyo teaches such knowledge.
...
It doesn't. Although in my opinion, it should.

ラーメン
STYLE
Wowww!
The salt in the soup is sparkling!
This place is amazing.
SLRRPP
体にやさし
無添加スープで
My body is absorbing all the umami from the chicken and vegetables...

Ohhh...
I'M SO FULL!
I didn't think we'd get 4 bowls just for lunch!
ARE YOU OKAY?
YAMMER
YAMMER
Fine!
OUR FAMILY RUNS TO BIG STOMACHS... WE GET THEM FROM MY GRANDMA.
MUNCH
MUNCH
...YOU'RE EATING TAKOYAKI *TOO?!*
YOU KNOW, IT'S OSAKA.

*Ahhh!*
NOW THAT I'VE HAD RAMEN, I REALLY WANT SOME SAKE!
KNOCK YOURSELF OUT.
*Figuratively or literally.*
...
BUT I WON'T.

...I QUIT MY JOB.
I'M MOVING TO TOKYO SINCE I HAVE RELATIVES THERE.
AND I'LL WORK THERE INSTEAD. SO THIS IS MY LAST DAY IN OSAKA.
YESTERDAY I WENT OUT DRINKING WITH MY FRIENDS...
WHY'D YOU QUIT? A NICE POSITION AT A BIG COMPANY! YOU'RE THROWING THAT AWAY...
But...
...THE DRINKING WASN'T ANY FUN.
THEN SUDDENLY IT CAME BACK TO ME...HOW I USED TO GO GET RAMEN AFTER DRINKING WITH MY FRIENDS WHEN I WAS YOUNG.
AND THAT'S WHEN I SAW YOU LAST NIGHT...
...AND I FELT YOUNG AGAIN... JUST EATING RAMEN TOO.

OKAY! THE WHITE SOUP AND THE SALT STYLES WERE GOOD, BUT YOU CAN'T BEAT THE OLD *SHOYU* FLAVOR! YEAH, SOY SAUCE IS THE FOUNDATION...

...WHEN I WAS IN SCHOOL, I USED TO GET IT AT A PLACE IN TSURUMI, BUT I DON'T REMEMBER WHERE EXACTLY. IT HAD NARUTO ON TOP.

Naruto as in the surimi, not the manga. Manga would get soggy if you put it on top of ramen.

...

I KNOW THE PLACE YOU'RE THINKING OF.
Now I want it, too.
REALLY?
Thanks!


中華そば

THIS IS THE PLACE, BUT...

...IT'S *NOT* IN TSURUMI ...?

...

Sorry. It's been a while since I was in school.

ACTUALLY...
...IT KINDA LOOKS LIKE ONE WE HAD BEFORE.
*Thanks for the meal.*
SLRRPP ちゅるるっ
MUNCH
UMM?

BUT THIS WAS IT!
THIS LIGHT, SIMPLE CHINESE NOODLE STYLE *CHUKA-SOBA!*
YOUR MEMORIES WERE CORRECT. THE ORIGINAL STORE MOVED FROM TSURUMI TO HERE A FEW YEARS AGO.
Confusingly, they also have a second location... in Tsurumi.
THANK YOU FOR CLEARING THAT UP.

...

EVEN WHEN YOU MOVE TO A NEW PLACE, THE TASTE IS THE SAME!

THE LAST RESTAURANT IS LOCATED IN AN OFFICE AREA.

乾杯!

KOIZUMI-CHAN, YOU'RE MEAN TO TAKE ME AROUND HERE.

*I told you I just quit my job...*

I JUST WANTED TO TRY THE BLACK RAMEN THEY SERVE HERE BEFORE I GO BACK TO TOKYO.

*Nothing personal.*

STARE

BY THE WAY...

I THOUGHT YOU DIDN'T DRINK WHEN YOU'RE EMOTIONAL.

Um...

...BUT YOU SEE, THIS HERE IS RURI, THE PURE PREMIUM PILSNER FROM COEDO BREWERY. IF IT'S ON THE MENU, I CAN'T PASS IT UP.

あははっ A HA HA

...

...WHAT I'M TRYING TO SAY IS...

I MEAN...

GULP! GULP! GULP!
GULP! GULP! GULP!
HAHHHHH
I'VE LIVED IN THIS CITY FOR 25 YEARS...
...AND I'M JUST ABOUT TO START A NEW LIFE SOMEWHERE ELSE.
HERE I AM, WITH A CUTE GIRL LIKE YOU...
...JUST HAVING SOME AMAZING RAMEN...
...AND I'M NOT EMOTIONAL, BUT...

...YOU KNOW...
...I FEEL SO GOOD NOW!!
AND ALSO...

I QUIT MY JOB BECAUSE I WANTED TO KEEP WORKING IN THE LONG RUN.
It wasn't a bad move for my career overall.
世界一暇なラーメン屋
The most desarted Ramen-Bar in the world...
ISN'T THAT CONTRA-DICTORY?
Well...
...IN ADULT LIFE, THERE ARE CONTRA-DICTIONS EVERY-WHERE.

ANY-WAY...
...THANKS FOR THE MEAL.

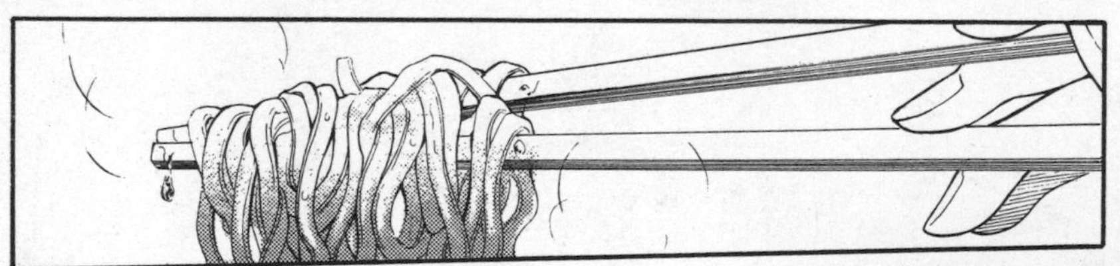

UMMMMMMM....!
SOO-OOO GOOD!
See...
...RAMEN NOODLES ARE THE ONE KIND OF TANGLES YOU CAN ENJOY.
The rest, maybe you just gotta move away from.
?

A few days later

Behold! Kinryu Ramen in Dotonbori... and the legendary dragon who protects Osaka!
(lie)
Ayane (14 years old)
Look, look! There's a dragon on top of that ramen shop!
That's so cool! Hey, what's up, dragon...?!
Shu (8 years old)
Yu (5 years old)
wave!
wave!

Ms. Koizumi loves ramen noodles

AFTER THE RAINY SEASON WAS OVER, MS. KOIZUMI CAME DOWN WITH A COLD.

SHE WAS SO SICK THAT SHE STARTED MISSING CLASS...

## 27th Bowl: Reunion

...AFTER TWO WEEKS AWAY.

ザワ
CHATTER
CHATTER
ザワ
See ya!
What are you up to after school?
STEP STEP
スタ スタ
Eh?!
YU, AREN'T YOU GONNA WALK HOME WITH KOIZUMI ...?
YOU HAVEN'T SEEN HER IN A LONG TIME.
What's wrong?
YES, I KNOW. BUT NOT TODAY...
HUH? WHY?!
What hap-pened?
Um...
I WAS GONNA ASK HER...
BUT...
MS. KOIZUMI! LET'S GO HOME TOGETHER!
I'm glad you're well! ♥
NO, THANK YOU.
Don't be shy!
LET'S GET RAMEN TO CELEBRATE YOUR RECOVERY!

RA-
MEN...
AFTER SHE GOT SICK...
...MS. KOIZUMI COULD HARDLY EAT ANYTHING.
I REALIZED...
...SHE NEEDS SOME TIME TO HERSELF.
TODAY IS THE FIRST DAY SHE CAN HAVE RAMEN AGAIN...AFTER SO LONG...
HERE'S YOUR *CHUKA SOBA!* THANK YOU FOR WAITING.

TIE
ぎゅっ
...
TAP
SLRRPP
ずずずっ

GULP
ごくん

KRIKK
パキッ

GRAB
くいっ

FWOOO
ふー
FWOOO
ふー

SLLRRPP
ちゅるっ

MUNCH
もぐっ
MUNCH
もぐっ
MUNCH
もぐっ
MUNCH
もぐっ

CHEW
もぐ
CHEW
もぐ

CHEW
もぐ
CHEW
もぐ
...

ぐぐっ
PULLL
PULLLL
ズズズズズ
SSSLLLRRRRRPPPPPP

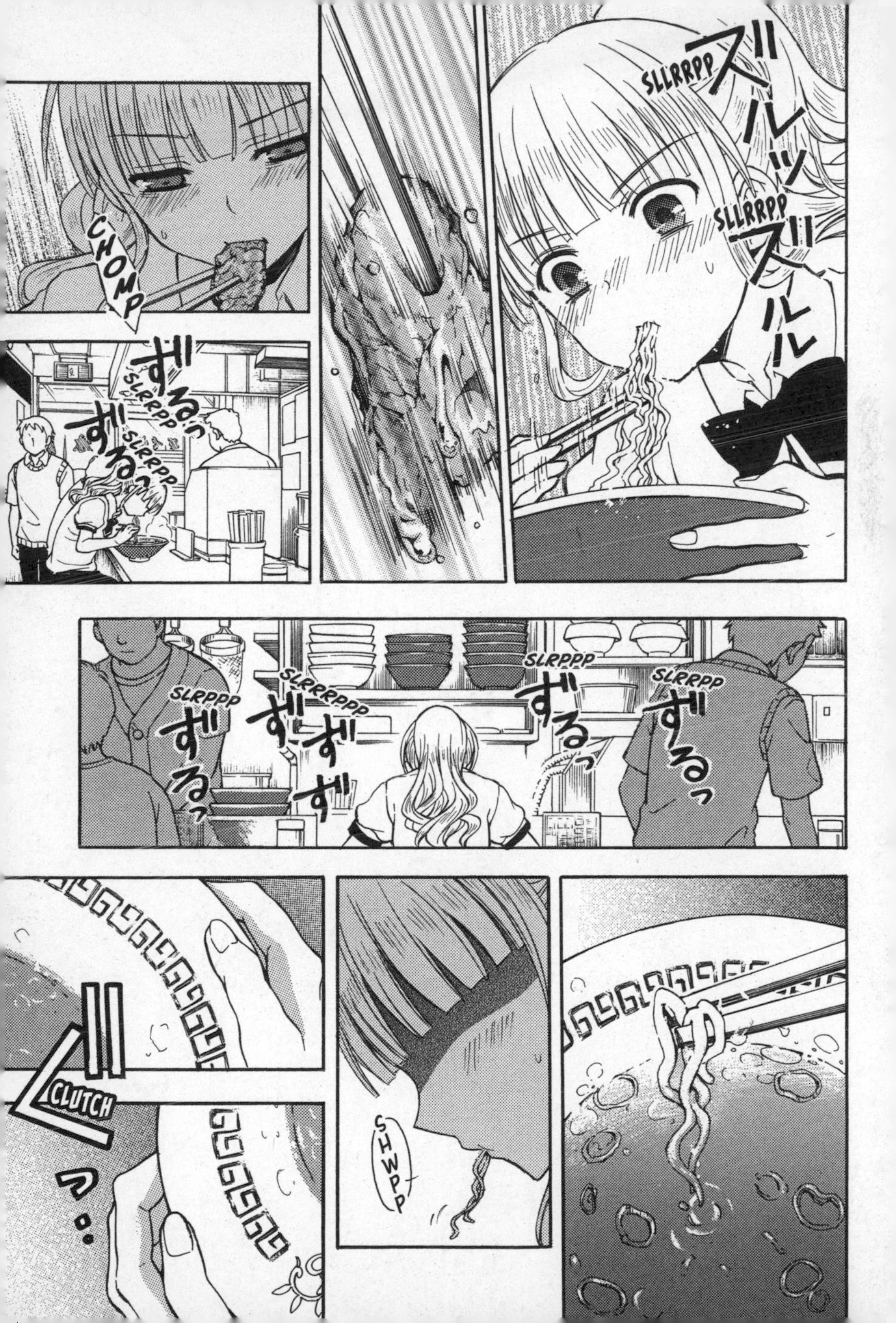

ズルッ
SLLRPP
ズルル
SLLRPP
CHOMP
ずるっ
SLRRPP
ずるっ
SLRRPP

ずるっ
SLRPPP
ずるっ
SLRPPP
ずずずず
SLRRRPPPP
ずるっ
SLRPPP

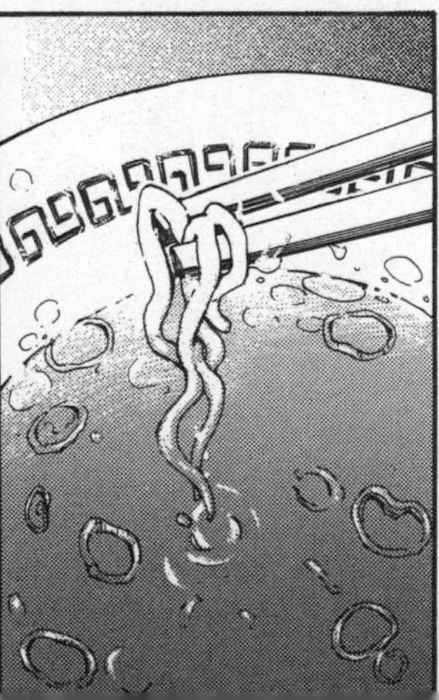

SHWPP

CLUTCH

DRIP
DRIP

GULP
GULP
GULP
GULP
GULP
GULP
GULP
GULP
GULP
GUULPP...
SMAK
HAHHHHH...

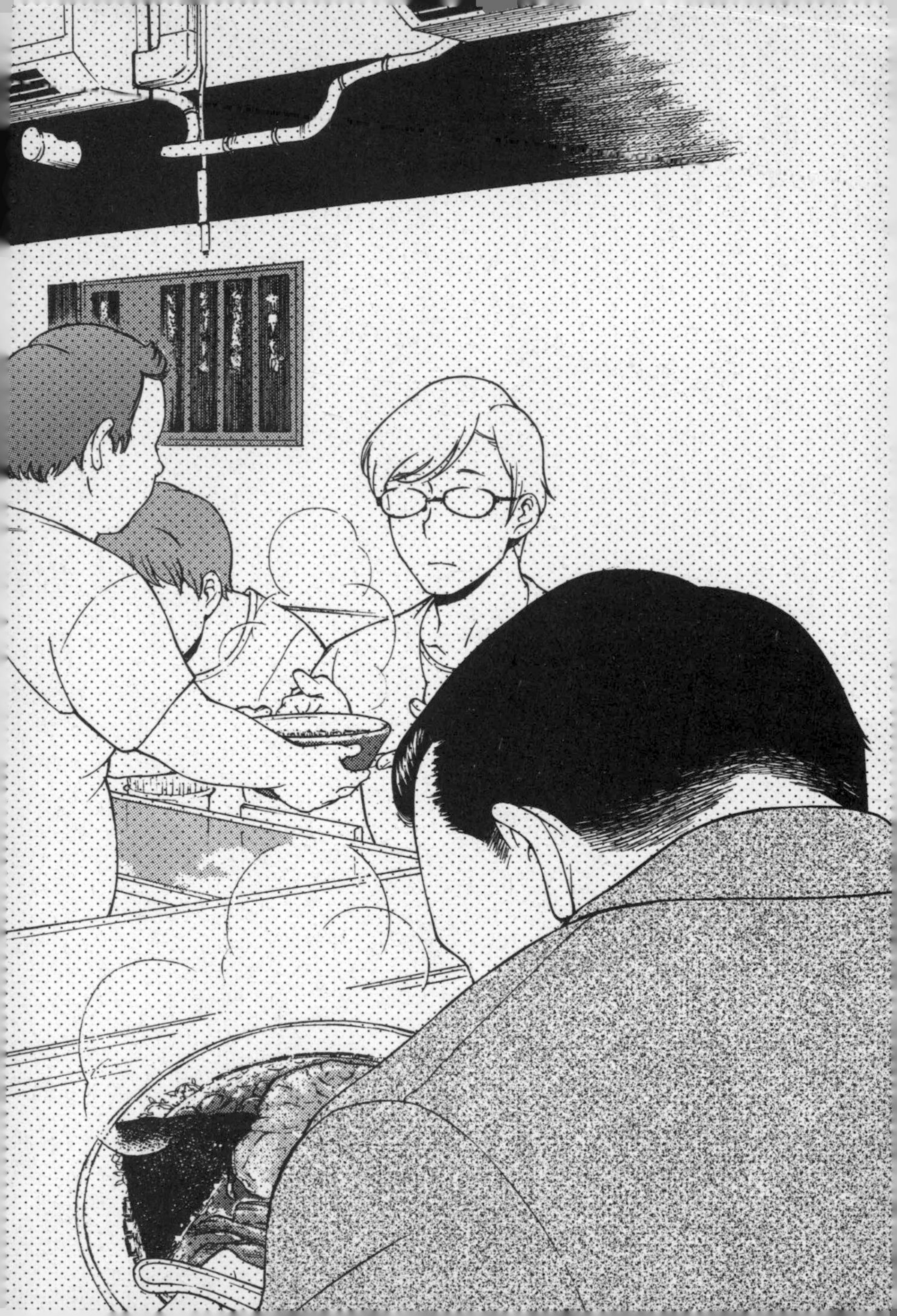

はー…
SIGHHHHHHHH

I'M SO GLAD, MS. KOIZUMI....

She stalked her anyway!

Yes, but WE stalked her stalking, so I'm not sure if we have the moral high ground.

STARTING TOMORROW...

...I'LL BE BY YOUR SIDE AGAIN... MS. KOIZUMI WHO LOVES RAMEN NOODLES.

SHIVER
ぶるっ
…
I still feel cold a little.

We've been getting some reader questions about Ms. Koizumi.
What does she think about dipping your noodles?
What's her first name?
Where's she from?
How tall is she?
Does she have any family?
What are her measurements?
What type of...guy... does she like?
....
You'll get no answers in vol. 4.
Wait, dipping noodles? Okay, so...

* Readers, please remember...Ms. Koizumi is one of those mysterious transfer students!

## p o s t s c r i p t

If you are reading this book then that means Vol. 3 has been published. I don't know what to say but THANK YOU! Thank all of you who have been reading our books.

Let's briefly recap the ramen I've had this past year.

From winter to spring, I was so deeply into back fat ramen. I don't know why, but I kept coming back to it. In summertime I was into *abura soba* (ramen without the broth, but with the sauce and fat) and simple *chuka soba* (Chinese chicken noodle style). After eating lighter ramen for months, now that it's the fall season, I want to eat something rich. This volume reflects my recent eating trips to Osaka. As I write this, it's September, which means I only have three months left in the year to eat ramen. I'm hoping I can get away to the north for noodles on my next trip.

Did you know that *Ms. Koizumi Loves Ramen Noodles* also became a live-action TV series on Fuji TV? It's true! Actress and model Akari Hayami, who got her start in Momoiro Clover, played Ms. Koizumi, and I am very happy to hear that many of the reviews are quite good. It's all thanks to the people who worked so hard on the production of this TV drama! Maybe some of you even discovered this manga because of the series. With all the support I'm getting, I really can't wait to write the next volume!

I'll do my best to make Vol. 4 a success!

—naru narumi

twitter:
@naruminaru3
I'll tweet about *Ms. Koizumi* there!

Osaka is famous for food such as *takoyaki* (grilled, seasoned balls of batter filled with minced octopus), *okonomiyaki* (a thick savory crepe) and, *tessa* (sashimi from *fugu*, the infamous deadly blowfish). But more than anything, it's famous for ramen! Ramen's very hot in Osaka these days, so let's check out some shops whose very names have an Osaka style to them!

## Tsuiteru Nakayama

It means "With Good Luck Nakayama," and with a name like this, the shop is sure to have good fortune! It's about a two minute walk west from Takii station on the Keihan Main Line. This restaurant features the same chicken soup with Chinese noodles that originated at Osaka's famous Kadoya Shokudo ramen shop (where the owner trained). Tsuiteru's noodles are very curly and are served with a light soup. It's a very traditional Chinese noodle (*chuka soba*) style.

FUSUMA-NI KAKERO NAKAZAKI-ICCHOU

## Nakazaki Shoutengai 1-6-18-Gou Ramen

About two minutes' walk northeast of Nakazakicho station on the Osaka Metro Tanimachi Line. This is what people mean by shops with "Osaka style" names—weird even by Japanese standards. This restaurant's actual full name sounds like text on a business card, beginning with the motto, *Fusuma-no Kakero*—"Bet On The Bran"—followed by the shop's address, and then, well, the word "ramen." A lot of Japanese just call it "Fusumakake" for short. But as for the bran, that refers to what goes into the flour of the special noodles made here. It's whole-grain goodness, fitting perhaps for a neighborhood like Nakazakicho, where you can get multiple varieties of homemade organic granola (at La Granda Familio).

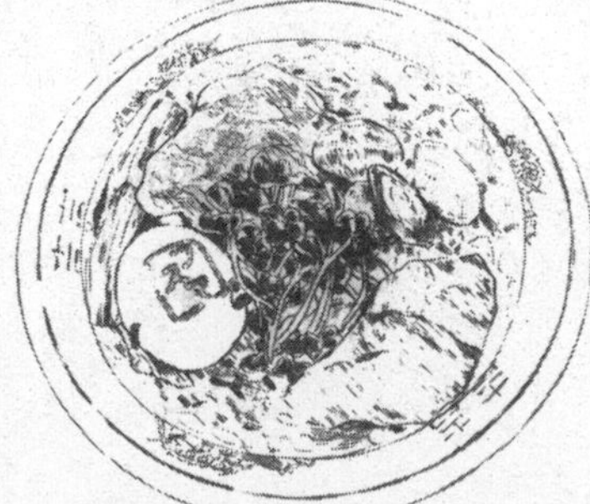

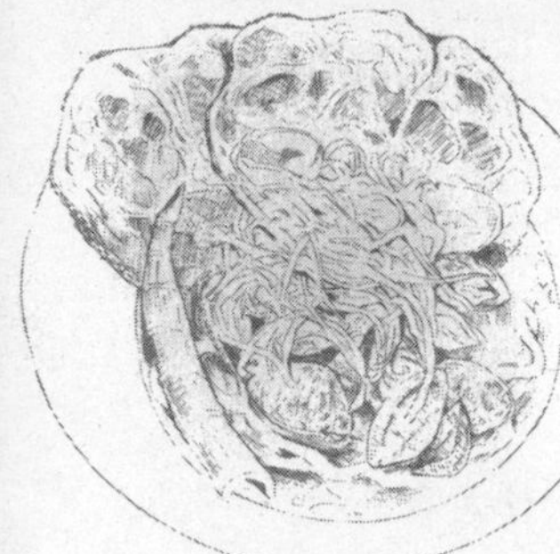

## Kuso-oyaji Saigono Hitofuri

"A Shitty Dad's Last Swing" is what it means, and be reminded again that you are dining in Osaka, where people not only say what they feel, they put it up on their storefront. But there's nothing—er—crappy about the taste of the soup here, a classic blend of shoyu and clam broth. It's less than a minute's walk west of the multi-line Juso station. Part of a chain that keeps you on your toes by all having different names—its other locations include Jinrui Mina Menrui ("The Human Race is All Noodles") and Sekai-ichi Himana Ramen-ya ("The Most Deserted Ramen Bar in the World").

This time, I ordered *take* which, as the name suggests, comes with very thick *menma* (bamboo shoots). The soup is made from many different root vegetables, and made me think of *nikomi* udon (udon cooked in the pot) because of its light, mild nature. It's good to have when your stomach needs a break. When you add some ginseng vinegar to the soup, it gets even lighter and more refreshing.

You'll have to excuse me, but I hadn't actually developed much of an impression of Osaka ramen until recently. It was only in the past few years that I began to slowly but surely feel its power. It wasn't too long ago that I went to a ramen event in Tokyo, and tried some ramen varieties from Osaka there—and they blew me away!

Eventually, I made a pilgrimage to Osaka that included local chains, old-school shops, and hipster joints. All were amazing. I started off at random with Kinguemon—I mean, it's in Dotonbori, and you can't get more Osaka than that. I had the Osaka Black style, with its rich soy flavor (actually, black style is found nationwide in Japan, but it's different in each region).

I also tried many different *chuka soba* style places, like Tsuiteru and Kadoya Shokudo—a style I got addicted to. Even after I came back to Tokyo, I remained into this light ramen for quite a while. Osaka ramen is like being dealt a hand of wild cards—you never know what new cool ramen you'll get into when you visit there.

In the end, though, I thought I should try *something* in Osaka other than the ramen, so I had a burger and fries at the Tenichi in Kire-uriwari. You'll remember Ms. Koizumi having one in vol. 1, p. 50. And just like Ms. Koizumi, I had it with some ramen.

naru narumi

president and publisher **Mike Richardson**

editor **Carl Gustav Horn**

lettering and retouch **Susie Lee**

designer **Anita Magaña**

digital art technician **Ann Gray**

*english-language version produced by dark horse comics*

**Ms. Koizumi Loves Ramen Noodles Vol. 3**



Published by
Dark Horse Manga
A division of Dark Horse Comics LLC
10956 SE Main Street
Milwaukie, OR 97222

DarkHorse.com
To find a comics shop in your area visit comicshoplocator.com

First edition: April 2021
ISBN 978-1-50671-329-8
10 9 8 7 6 5 4 3 2 1
Printed in the United States of America

# Here's how you do it!

*Ms. Koizumi Loves Ramen Noodles*, like most manga, is read in the traditional Japanese style, right-to-left, so turn the book around to begin. Please do not attempt to slurp this manga.